sip slow and prosper

Publisher s Cataloguing-in-Publication data

sip slow and prosper : poetry / dylan brooks

author: brooks, dylan
editor: dallong, deegy
designer: parke, linda
illustrator: dunlop, sarah
production: brooks, dylan

ISBN: 978-1-7774827-0-1 (print)
ISBN: 978-1-7774827-6-3 (e-book)

subjects: LCSH Canadian poetry--21st century.

classification: LCC PS3602.R S 2022 | DDC 811.6--dc23

http://www.brooksdylan.com

for
the lost and found
the ashamed and proud
the caged and unafraid
the silent and sound and
those coming around
everlastingly
for
my family

contents

arrival

it can be difficult living
in the periphery of *why* and *how*

why begs questions from choices
our unseen reasons

how is coloured
by accounts of then and now

with a foothold for my thoughts
i wrote something down.

inward

"the passing hours had a strangeness to them, loose and unstructured, as though the stitches were broken, the tent of time sagging one moment, billowing the next."

rohinton mistry – *a fine balance*

loose ends

facing east
on a westward shore

one lighthouse away
from the last

the more i explore
big rock to willow point

the further that red door.
what resides behind is painful to endure

an unmarked beginning
now impossible to ignore

life before these mountains
a truth disguised in folklore

one to address and set free
some day – i'm sure.

self-conscious

we need quiet places
to be our loudest self

to sing and not shout –
an exploration of who

and what we're all about.
soul

without a doubt
let it all out.

expectations

sitting at home
with your hat on the shelf
you expect big things of yourself
and sometimes everybody else.

you tell stories of turtles without shells
dwelling each night to the same spell

stop!
snap back from this attack
kick the facts and stay on track
to where it all started –

when your shoulders didn't sag
and those heels never dragged.

fix your hat
live for today in any which way
have your say –
stay peaceful and out of the fray.

anxious

otherworldly bliss
in this sun-kissed happiness

yet under the surface
winds begin to shift
tides tend to drift –

thoughts once vast
now too specific.
i can't help but take a breath –

keep with it
hold on and don't slip.

acknowledge > < dismiss

to think a thought
don't rush the plot

somewhere along the way
i forgot

what was hot-to-trot
came full stop.

to think a thought
from dot jots to mental block

searching for sweet spots
in bountiful crops of language.

to think a thought
at the banquet of anguish

watch as my words form clots
under this heavy blanket.

to allow all thoughts
without judgement –

even what's considered naught
might be the adjustment i need

to carry out
this pause.

apprehensive

to seek joy
as a nervous boy

in a shell
of dreams.

trust fall

to believe in more than you know
are you willing to go?

to be steadfast or rock slow
into the unknown

blind faith
the idea of letting go

fearful
to show a latent trust in the day

are you even capable
to remain

or slowly grow
into the obtainable?

steadfast

be true as the ocean blue
the clues are within you

if not now
soon.

ready or not

where candid thoughts are measured
if you're ready or not –
are you steady enough to express
the colours of your plot?

in a place that makes us question
why we can't be ourselves
who are they to say
what comes and goes off the shelf?

i respond more each day
by letting more of me out
with every reveal i feel less doubt

an idea or even a sound –
insecurities shout from under my skin
as if to say *why would you go do that now?*

can't i just be myself in this vulnerability?
looking into mirrors or back at crowds
without judgement weighing me down.

in a place i need to embrace my being
i found meaning
but they seem to know more –
though other lives are easier to explore.

is that why they pick through mine?
a box is not the space for open thoughts
have you noticed time doesn't stop –
or rain falls the same way it drops?

stuck in an office full of clocks
trying to find the inspiration i forgot.

where i need to be

i need to be
the versions of me

in order for me to see
and believe

in the person
and places i want to be.

quest

i woke up playing pretend again
to what end i don't know
torn between poems and a payroll.

who made the white collar
professional
and why can their players pass go?

to pay mind instead of rent
when can i get my cheque?

what comes next is something to stress
the notion causes me to vex

who do i want to be
and where will i step?

all i want to be is my best
but this desk
burns a hole in my chest

i'm looking for a sign
and nothing less.

signs

driving highway three
surrounded by a day old scene
pastel pines and lakesides
copper mountain in my periphery.

in the late summer heat
what lays ahead of me is a mirage

my future displaced above asphalt
waving towards the sky.
i'm beginning to believe in forces unseen
without questioning why

hiding behind this failing windshield
doing 105 from an idle mind.

no longer can i pretend –
suddenly i see
the sign that reads *hope*
110 kilometers ahead.

envision

my eyes feel awake today
pointed at the pie in the sky
except it's facing the ground

i'm wearing crust for a crown.
thinking how life passes us by
like *waldo* in crowds

if we're more lost than found.
find us at twenty six degrees
in this half-baked dream

what i choose to believe
is becoming part of me
i am my own destiny.

wabi-sabi

admiring tidelines
like timelines

low and high
open and entwined

such is life
even on cloud nine.

ponderings #4

suburban mood swings
and other things

chameleon skies meld
self-love and acceptance

i stand on the toe of this driveway
watching houses fade from grey
into vibrant transcendence –

clouds coloured by setting suns
roll along the ridgelines
of a muted suburbia.

fleeting words

the words i haven't said yet
how can i fumble on what i can't forget?

words of sincerity
of meaning

of how you make my chest leap
while it lays to rest

before i can speak
my heart cashes cheques at the bank of hesitation

waiting for the moment
to express terms of adoration

what if i sign the line in desperation
to feel accepted

beloved
and look after?

oh to know what's real and unprotected
in this open field

the words i have not said in this chapter
are better sung to you

behind the veil
of everything we do

at the tip of tied tongues
in the kick of beating drums

some days the words i have to say
want to up and walk away

wouldn't it be nice if they stayed?
i could name a few

but until the moment
what's the use?

holding back

caged and afraid
the music wants to play

i'm all too cautious
another fool in the rain

in time
the noise will have its day

the sound will find its way
my voice will set the stage.

life's composition

down in the *port of morrow*
up before beggars borrow
trading my shakes for shine
and sun rays for sorrow.

minutes pass like hours
by and by i realize
she was always mine
despite our petty crimes

in spite of harder times
i have to believe
orbiting stars eventually align
and the universe shows signs.

down in the port of *burrard*
what i feel this morning
resides between these lines
and the hollow of a guitar.

identity swing

looking for a symbol
in these cymbals

i'll ride
until i crash

searching for a message
in this riddle

often times it's just me
in the middle

dreaming big
when i'm feeling little.

imposter

i'm late for work today
(slow to go)

something i've come to know
standing in the shadow
of tomorrow

thinking faster than i can act
keeping me from things i aspire
and long to attract –

purpose and all that.
all this weight on my back

is starting to stack
and it must slough
if i intend to stay on track.

in my own home
feet planted with thoughts overgrown –

draped over the couch
where they'll stay
for a night or a few days.

tangled and uncombed
too stoned and ashamed

my monkey mind
won't stop or refrain
in its fits and starts –

ideas arrive in a hurry
to be hosed from my heart.

inspiration sparks
only to be doused in whole
or in part.

get out of your way

in the rubble of my mind
i unpack things one at a time
like search and rescue
but i'm walking the line

calling out to survivors
to surrender what i find.
day after day
night after night

putting away wrongs
to make a few right –
my thoughts
are getting tight.

there's nothing to see
and i can't beg a dime –
how deep the ocean can be
without a guide

underwater i close my eyes
to take another look inside.
foraging for truth in a current of lies

changing tides sweep me
in an upwelling of some type
i rise back to the surface –
thrashed with purpose and life.

alignment

i've been working through old refrains
trying to make space for new pathways
you could say

in the transformation of change
we take only what we can pay –
like toll roads for closing lanes
or dry feet in the rain.

in this journey back to my natural state
i need to endure subtleties
with the pain of range

i'll reach until i stretch
my sleepy vertebrae –
when did i fall out of balance
and how do i centre back again?

head over heart over hip is the aim
i became prisoner in the weight
of my own vocation –
don't become one.

a job is a job and wage is wage
there's no shame in survival
but humans are meant to sustain

not by submitting claims
from benefits we loath to pay

cause of posture? sitting
cause of strain? same

create room for active energy
and ground this electricity
spread it out evenly –

we must learn to live
out of gravity.

spaces in between

equally important to sound
silence is a note of its own
a space to call home.

a room to ground down
and feel time coming around

how life eventually does.
with music and emotion
silence is synonymous.

we vary in the rhythms we carry
and though silence can be scary

its real power lies in delivery –
akin to small acts
of chivalry

silence is alive
as much as it is dead.

grey area

often transient and typical
the grey area of our lives prove pivotal
home of the hyphen
a spotlight for space and the invisible.

where discovery meets hysteria
on a bridge amid beginnings and ends
we find the grey area.

it was my twenty-fourth year
when i wet the feeling one last time –
loneliness felt before saying goodbye

sitting fireside
me myself and i
celebrating what was ahead
and all that was behind.

learning to be grateful
and how to stay aligned
although i didn't arrive

there alone
my worries of tomorrow
buried with a hatchet
letters burned so vengeance couldn't grab it.

then while smoking an old habit
i smudged the inside of my jacket
feeding my head with the luck of white rabbits

facing the accidents i had not yet forgiven –
and so there it was written.
in the heat of this disposition
to begin again i showed myself compassion.

sunset

come
around sundown

kiss the sea
and comb the clouds

make us feel
something we can't pronounce.

dawn of a new way

too many times
suppressing my mind
less triumph
more nosedives

half attempts
over self-made lies
now we're set to glide.

hold onto your pride
raise the masts
grab the strings
we sail at high tide.

the night's come alive
i'm down and a little shy
but all we can do is try –

still for now
i will standby

if you trust the wind
it'll teach you to fly
in the morning sky
we shall arrive.

belonging words

is it not strange?
the coincidence of words
how some come to arrange
naturally pleasant –
a revelation of the obscure.

poised to pronounce
right as rain
when the moment came

like a shadow to shade
two belonging words
pulled along imaginary string.

one through another
could make a quiet man sing
for nobody but himself –
the coincidence of words
is any but *one* thing.

perpetuate purpose

why do we write?
what is our purpose
and how will it serve
language using words?

the reasons are plenty
if they don't come empty

mine stem from the earth
seeded in storytelling
and all its worth –
honouring those who came first.

it's their lessons we must preserve
before data collection puts human connection
into a hearse –
traditions buried while history turns in the dirt.

let's return to love
and learn how love can just as easily hurt –

or we may fade like rhythm without a verse.
spoken words cannot go half heard or unfelt

what if all we had were stories?
i write to understand the versions of ourselves.

ourselves

meet me at the intersection
of *freedom* and *expression*

where "failures" no longer
need protection

we can be our *self* without
the daily lesson

no deflection here in the present.
no consequence for confidence
no explanation for your big step

the one you took on the corner of
chance and *happiness.*

wherever that is – you are yours now
find it in everyday practice
and don't become static

always love with tenderness
and be patient with the fanatic.

outward

"when familiar music filled her head, the past was conquered for a bri while, and she felt herself ache with the ecstasy of completion, as thoug a missing limb had been recovered."

rohinton mistry – *a fine balance*

ponderings #1

casting reflections
and snagging connections

river rocks roll
thunder beneath my feet

while i count souvenirs
better remembered than seen

casting a line
reeling in the years

missed relationships
wading through drying tears.

break the mold

people coming
people going

first impressions longing
with every conversation owing

on the streets of *vancouver*
they keep strolling
further from where i started
and you parted the sea –

each step tracing a life
i wasn't meant to believe.

there used to be four reasons
for the seasons i didn't create

too busy finding my way
until i found you –
in *robson square*
my heart spilt truth over gallery stairs

where my mind couldn't prove
what the stomach already knew.

outward

in choosing how to continue
the city was reduced –

from rail cars
cold bars and five string guitars
to the sound of shoes
tapping to the beat of all these

people coming
people going

lasting impressions growing
with every conversation due.

dearly departed

your dad left before you could develop a chest
one that now feeds a baby boy

it wasn't his intent to leave without his lesson
the sidewalk left him unable to speak

cold as the hospital
in which he fought until the end.

they say new life makes losing life
easier to understand

i hope you can defend the static in your head
mixed frequencies from the back room –

sometimes responsibility comes too soon.
i pray every day you survive each night

the older you get the further baby boy will step
in search of his own rights

where secrets are kept between love and regret.
in these moments will you learn to forgive

or live to forget?
will you always be his mother and nothing less?

all has yet to be read in the book of life
we believe in your best and *he* does too

should you need affirmation or proof
gaze into baby's brown eyes

be reminded of your roots.
realize the medicine in your dad's truth

ginaajiiw (you are beautiful)
nwaabdan enaazheyin (i see your light)

hold this feather
remember bears are stronger together.

fracture

"it's my dad's favourite song"

she said from the living room
if he only knew
how the tune played along her avenue

sometimes we can't look back
after everything we have been through.

mother's son

to the young lad on stage
curious soul uncaged

with a deep gaze
wild and un-phased

you stand there creating
from a blank page

someday you may not recall
with everything soon to change

our mothers pray we stay brave
in ways embers long to flame.

to the young lad making a name
go on and create waves

don't be quick to chase age
embrace this life with patience –

learn how to hold your hands
don't become complacent

keep moving mountains
in the joy of inspiration.

glorious awkwardness

glorious awkwardness
that wrenches our stomach
and tosses the chest

so many outlets
within awkwardness –
terror and regret circumvent

oh what it means to be human!
what do you think of when you reflect?

strangers or friends
past impressions or present tense

summer night sweats
or winter days stuck in bed –

if words found the voiceless
what do you think they would confess?

glorious awkwardness

ah yes
in an attempt to attach this thread
i must address my shyness

if you don't notice yet
listen when i resuscitate silence
with sound only to feel desperate.

only then do i see
spaces in between are necessary
for the moment –

"ah yes"
said the poet

glorious awkwardness

a necessary component
oh what it means to be human!

to live freely out in the open
can make more sense than spoken
learn to go with it when life's golden.

moment's unseen

often when we go to bed
my breath matches yours

riding the air you breathe
i never want to leave

this is catch
and release.

i listen to the beat of your chest
before returning to sleep

synchronized
and complete.

slow mornings

in the dawn
of today

a faint scent of coffee
spills into our bedroom

autumn falls from the hills
summer ended all too soon

darling i live to kiss
others to swoon

i lean in for another
on an everlasting thrill

you fill my heart
like wind to a mill

come along now
the morning's arrived

let's try on the day –
for you i will.

she moves me

something in the way
you brighten up my day

always close
never far away

two-tangled souls
we sway

stay

said the setting sky
you tell stories with your eyes
that make clouds cry
for joy and pain in the same line

rest

says the pounding in my chest
we have each other's best
the bullets of tomorrow won't
pierce this autumn harvest.

hold

as we embrace
where waves meet mountains

water and earth
chaos and order

this is love
without borders.

south of the border

sometime in october
we crossed state lines
and followed the coastal pine

painting our own poster
seaside in seattle –
where the air doesn't care

how many breaths you take
only the salt you're worth
and memories we make.

all i *see-at-all*
is a freedom of being
silent protests against the wall

in a city charmed with character
it's hard not to compare
vancouver or the feelings we share.

this story told by a visitor
is neither here nor there
the salish sea squares

our difference as far as i'm aware –
affordability and climate action
generational needs everywhere.

show me how

i've been looking
for you everywhere

on the edge of our bed
in the depths of my head –

you're out there somewhere.
caught up in a cloud
too afraid to look down

so read this scene.
in these states of affairs
should we dare to breathe –

do you even care i can't see?
the light in my eyes
returns to an untouchable sky

at what time will you arrive?
because the more i try
the less you want to know why

and that isn't easy for me –
watch these feelings override
i hope you choose to be mine.

sip slow and prosper

together we'll find motion
despite where we're going –
fill the voids calling out to you

i'll be the wind at your back
if you tell me what's wrong

is it panic
or too heavy to unpack?
we can leave it at that –

come down from your cloud now
the city's getting loud

we'll stack rocks until our silence
turns to sound –
if only you would show me how.

selflessness

with each stroke
her worrisome thumb

wore the rock smooth –
polished proud

with all
it had accomplished

for the good
it did her

by taking only a second
to put her first.

check-in often

it's been a week
we haven't taken tea

what will be will be
i'm lucky you're lovely

i know i can be here
i know i can be there

dancing around issues
or stacked between –
suffocating in open air.

my head shrouded by colossal thoughts
i'm always surrounded –
some days every move feels crowded

but you allow me to process
until we're grounded.

through the riff and raff
i know i can be this and that

and just before i crash
i'm saved by your laugh –
a sound i want to make last.

the high road

let's try not to fight
it could be our last night

the final flight
between right and wrong

let's live for more love songs
listen close and let yesterday belong

try to see something
in this acceptance

need nothing
seek peace of mind and penance

try and keep to your means
teach good deeds over greed

lower your weapons
and stand at ease.

lifelong dance

standing by the pier
radio static clings to our ears

thick smoke lingers on thin fabric
dust returns to the floor

beyond a screen door
reality turns to reminisce

like flat stones after they're skipped
we'll bounce further from our first kiss.

tonight's the night
before our history grows rich
with all the places we'll have been since

dancing one room to the next
midnight strikes six –

okanagan lake softens the shore.
music swings in 5/4 and it's so poetic

oh *mi amor*
let's never forget it.

comparison

we take too much
from ourselves

comparing experiences
until we're overwhelmed.

mysterious mental medium
why run lean and never lenient?

comparing to everyone else –
when has this been convenient?

people eventually see it
while best friends help reveal it

she believes in my achievement.
rest your head love

her voice sooths this moment
shielding me from the opponent.

conditions

in a society
conducive to adhd

how can we see
to our needs?

to look
to listen

to learn patience
for others and ourselves –

humanity
and everything else.

in a society
conducive to adhd

how can we *be* when greed
overcomes the needs of self?

conformance over awareness
in this obsolescence

clever distractions to ensure
we keep chasing the present.

in a society
conducive to adhd

how do we build a format
to not play the fool in combat?

death by comparison
in society's bait trap

take action in our condition
not favourable to that.

information age

waking up to a new day
in the information age

up up and away
you told me to come
but i wanted to stay.

yesterday
we were wild and free

departed from society
expectations –
what they wanted us to be.

today
brings different energy
our stimulation isn't sensory

there's more eyes than ears
poor taste and less touch
than previous years.

take back your own way
in the information age

to be brave
and confident again –
what of you will remain?

coming > < going

people talk of plans – perpetually
falling one into the other

propelling lots of plots and stops
before the calendar plays out

going without knowing
visiting without enjoying

what's another foot in these shoes?
what's an air-mile to a *boeing*?

are we being honest
or frenetically avoiding?

out of touch

in a world of smartphones
isn't it ironic?

we've grown dumb
over numb thumbs

disconnected by dial tones
keeping up only to stay low

it's getting harder to leave home –
to socialize or be alone?

a stone
to your glass dome

each day begs a new way
but to each their own

mind spent from self-contempt
who do you really know

in this information overload?
i say fuck that and the *fomo*

let's appeal for what's *real* –
not what you're told.

in a world of smartphones
allow yourself to let go.

black mirror

the advancement of society –
we as a whole

technology will automate
not only machine
but what's humanly if not careful.

in the twilight of our own defeat –
will it be an uncalculated mistake
or a risk not worth the debate?

emotional intelligence will slip
through our fingertips

global leaders won't be able to
grapple this shit

blinded by status and competition
in their deadly disposition –
if only the deception would listen.

i pace for the future
holding my breath inside poetry –

hoping we don't become
shelved like groceries.

ponderings #2

life's a zoo
mind your *p's* and *q's.*

in the rat race of life
what's better –
to be crude or kind?

for everyone we meet down the line
can be the end or start of something new

upon a fresh slate who are you?
to lead with ignorance
or challenge your social purview?

in spite of what you don't know
and all you once knew.

layover

pre-boarding
post boredom

on my way
to kingdom come

two fists stretched to the sun
one raised for love –

the other locked in luck.
thirsty palettes urge unbroken glass

memories are said to last
before they're done

steel birds soar soft skies
weighing next to none

my thoughts return from space –
a brief layover from the human race

fuck
middle seat – "e" twenty-one.

voyage

i'm tired of emails reaching dead ends
like drying ink to a pen
i can't pretend to be stuck here again
because i am

gravity won't save me
like it did back then
why can't i take all this red
and give up the gold instead?

press it into a book of all the words
i have ever shed –
formed into beautiful lines
from the whirlpool in my head

that would be worth the minutes
of my day – everything said.

walking the line between hesitation
and action
when the moment gains traction
i want it to be just right

not where i once left it
but in my fists clenched tight
humbled departures into my next life
where i own the stones to my appetite.

between dreams

have you ever been caught
between dreams

living
out of the in-seam
contrary beliefs sewn
from juggling two journeys?

i know
the feeling

the first falls typical
a journey in the artificial

unseen by the mystical
challenged as cynical –
another cog
in the machine.

the second is personal
a world of your own

one made of less material
and more heartfelt creation

made by you for you
in the spirit of preservation

cite the child's imagination
where inspiration
feeds your dedication –
what will you choose to be?

in between dreams
will passion meet vocation?

campaign trail

i wake up with the sun
shining on the same block

ready to punch this clock
for the hands that don't stop.

i walk with my shadow –
questions plateau every thought

under the hands that won't stop
over the township plot.

to trust in community
built by a sea of green

where policies dictate the means
agendas shuffle like restless feet –

to repeat history without change
another ring in the tree of strange

growing pains felt before they came
what's my vote in their campaign?

division > < distraction

in the parliamentary promise
of a new day

high above another inversion
of challenge –

of change.
how can *we* be certain

when everything remains
the same?

more than meets the eye

rolling rocks into the sea
thinking how can it be –
beyond the trees
a forest so green

behind the screen
a reality unseen
both beautiful and ugly

there's more to our taught history
than you and me
textbooks don't mention heroes
like *teit* – *marsha* – *aoki*

why can't we read
truths buried underneath
the same glossed over bigotry?

rolling rocks into the sea
thinking how can reality
remain –
century after century?

privileged and uneducated

my elbows are rooted to
the kitchen table

i ramble against society
and its oppression –
finding humanity lost
without stable direction

head in hand
these words won't stand

my education is outside
with the homeless man
screaming "the system's broke!"
a campaign backed by beer cans

frustrated
i begin to understand

i stop to listen of people and partitions
systemic issues no longer hidden –
why should anyone have to fight
for civil rights as a citizen?

we need to act now
as a coalition

stop
think –
band together
if not for you then for the children

take a chance on your world view
why wouldn't you?

challenge your inner politician –
everything we thought we knew
we need to hear
the truth.

moral crossroad

we're going to do what we're going to do
so who are you?

in a moment of truth
would you speak up or stash the proof?

remember
only good for good it can do.

small worlds

small worlds collide
on a constant unjust ride
tearing away social fabrics
like governments over land rights

humanity has to decide
to live or let die
at this intersection we all cry
pushing between the wall and its lies.

i'm tongue-tied in shame
the plight and pain of political games
stifling change for a new way –
we can't allow the future to die in vain

how naive we've chosen to be
enabling greed on oppressed dreams –
forgetting we are of one species
joined at the hip of reality.

to be human is to respect yourself
and the neighbourly –
a commandment you see
to be free and friendly

we need to live in love
and make peace
a lifetime is temporary
for everybody.

ponderings #3

deep in the trout creek meadow
lay steep embankments

water weaves its way in fragments
toward the fertile lake afar.

overhead a steam train operation –
thirty years since it left the station

tired tracks rest upon a figuration
of evenly spaced steel

bridging the built and natural world
now ours to heal.

climate unchanged

time spent and money kept
what is a green spirit's lament
in a city no slyer than slicker?

be quick to scale this *richter*
the magnitude is hard to deliver
when the jury's out for something bigger

with one finger in the little dipper
i'm searching for a cause
while life on mars chokes back a snicker.

two tickets to the show
they call irony
or spin the globe

what do you figure –
how far will humankind go?
the toll to consider is elemental

companies scabbing earth for gold
trading compassion for payroll
inching closer to *her* threshold.

in this generational gap
good intentions are said to relapse
before they too are sold

our common ground is environmental.
perhaps if i write a letter in all caps
it might put *her* cries on the map

god only knows if we do
we'll reach an impasse –
one they'll find ways to tax

why try in the first place?
go ask the junk
orbiting in outer space

captive on a carousel of crime
how much more will it take
before *she* runs out of time?

trees before discovery

in the eye of an old oak
seize the air i breathe
touch my lobed leaves
swing from every branch i sweep

learn the walloping dance i teach.
in nature my knowledge is preached
another day i believe
water lies beyond the other trees

how long has my life been?
years – *no* – centuries
since i've seen the roots to my feet
buried deep by now

i wonder
under this brown sodden earth
if only i could reach inside
and count the rings to my girth

quickly –
i can hear industry creeping
my neighbours start weeping
"hey! we were here first!"

stuck screaming
while humans get to work
all i wanted to be was appreciated
but not in this world of hurt –

back into the soil from which i came
a seed in the dirt of *mother's* name
she will nurture me for what i am
an oak who would rather stay.

fight or flight

what will you say
when there comes a day

to go
the other way?

in the heat of difference
what will you say?

in the defining moment
will you walk or will you stay?

window

sometimes i can't see past the day
my eyes have grown tired and my gaze astray
somehow all of this goes away
when i sit by my favourite window

watching the world and its ways
unfolding through the same pleasant pane –
one that sees the sun as it feels the rain.

today the morning sky calls for rays
it's early and i'm up with the birds
they seem to be the first to rise
i sing back so they feel heard.

their sounds wrap around my senses
lifting my mouth to form a smile
i call this mending the fences
or returning my inner child.

in the distance stand three tall giants
snow-covered and defiant
they stand in silence

humbling the cities at its feet
made of evergreens and river streams
we call these mountains *beings*.

towering ridges reach for the clouds
striking the blue background
where earth meets wind –

scars hint a glacial movement
trails run through trees
to where our built world begins.

(two years later)

construction continues to reshape this view
i have a month until new apartments eclipse
what the crews can't undo

hammering away until they're paid
this is why i rise day after day –
in pursuit of quiet hours
i won't have again.

once we're wrapped in glass
and the last slab has cured in place
rentals will take what i used to appreciate

though it's not the end of nature's brigade.
squirrels will scurry across power lines
i will still hurry for the *break-a-dawn*
to grab at falling time –

such fine sand in a closed palm
i'm molding these moments
before they're gone.

leaf sound shelf

slow your roll
and save yourself
place your hat on a shelf
for nobody else
except your well-being

seeing hardly – softly listening
restoring our meaning
in this park after dark
two hearts beating.

without speaking
night thoughts steal today away from her
i've come to learn we can't play
when we're still healing –
kiss the breeze until these feelings return

slow your roll
and save yourself
it's time to accept your version of help –
remember trees fall and all
except in good health

small details to forget
under a sweeping leaf
while we lay among fleeting sounds –
quiet in our state of retreat.

mindfulness interrupted

it's contradictory –
the idea of staying present

mindful
in the moment

to achieve this in a society
tailored to results
one that dresses up insults.
for lack of efficiency

what we need is our pulse
and a soothing frequency
to cultivate positivity
without the negativity

imagine the possibilities
if we prioritized our ability
to stay present –
mindful in the moment.

if we learned how
by playing chess with our breath

each cycle a calculated sequence
of nothing more and everything less.

impermanence

a letter to the editor
it's better we don't address each other
this is patience to the go-getter

checking today's weather –
sunshine without stressors
have you met her?

my skin's soft but strong as leather
try harder
if you think you're clever

however
what tethered me down
will soon wash away –

ode to all the matter
in constant state of change
before this passive feeling caves

just remember
no position is permanent
in an existential daze –

we're made to *form* then *fade.*

depth over distance

in a clash of generations
the *twentieth* is in disbelief
believing neither you or me
grieving what used to be rudimentary

lost capabilities
on those from generation *y-z*
too focused on worth
without putting in the work

the one written on every sin card
seven numbers to which we stick.
pillars of knowledge
stand over millennials like monoliths

i'm sick of the shallow waters
between us and them
information continues to hurry
in and out of conversation

continually buzzing
from nation to nation.
we've traded quality for quantity
then bragged about the changes –

sip slow and prosper

facts left unchecked
but we have to face it
this is distance without depth
multimedia addictions unkempt

let's celebrate whoever's left
in tradition of deeper ponds
before the storytellers pass
and a way of understanding is gone.

be curious

we are of the questions we ask

i repeat

we are of the questions we ask.

returning to our elders

a few words to the wiser
it seems age is a lender
of time in the end

hand after hand after hand
clocks melt away like sand

now that i'm older
understanding
blew through the window

whispering winds brought me
back to you

with a heart-full of questions
i have yet to ask
though i always meant to.

in learning how
i've been more slow than proud

would you believe
the night sea
gifted me eyes and ears?

when i ask of life and years
i will listen for your laugh
and watch how you persevered.

yin and yang

what would you say
if tomorrow took today
away from where we stay
and the bed we lay –
what could you say?

does it all seem the same
frisco without the bay
the mind without a state
thoughts to an endless tape –
what should you say?

can you live for the moment
or will you pump the brakes
to let go or keep the faith
within your heart space?

does everything come at a trade
will only the sun bring us shade
can acceptance be without blame
what is tomorrow beyond today

what if we were already made?
omnipresent in every way
do we need to say
anything – anything at all.

along the way

the crease in your shirt
shows healing
where it used to hurt

when you sang for change
and were quick to revert

but today –
something
tastes pivotal and great

your silence will break
and confidence will stay

you worked hard
to illuminate
this new mind state –

learned to stack smaller crates
balancing a life to celebrate.

upward

"he smiles because he is constantly afloat in the love of the Divine Mother. tears of ecstasy soak his eyelashes"

kay larson – *where the heart beats*

ode to the late bloomer

ode to the late bloomer
don't worry *this* didn't happen sooner

you're doing fine
just remember all phases are not lunar
and most stars can't shine.

to reassure of how and why
is to say you'll catch every train on time

in this life
you are what you try
don't waste a heart to satisfy the mind

push on
and soon enough you'll arrive.

empowered

i woke up early on my birthday
i'm twenty-seven
in this lesson

my adolescence leads
a winding road to the present
but this time i'm not stressing

they say don't give
when you should be getting

if you have a minute
i'll only take a second

let me freshen my impression
take no shit for suggestion

on the north side of twenty
i walk my own direction.

make space

if it's faith you lust
and religion is a bust
who can you trust?

do what you must
but don't take too much
try giving less a fuck

slow down
don't rush
your voice won't be hushed.

what's true unto you
will light your days to come
so real to the touch.

you glow
like steel railways
under a setting sun

this is self trust
in a sudden cold crush
guiding you home.

law of dreams

the journey of rain
from a bursting cloud
changes shape
while matter showers down.

what is this all about?
the matter –
grimly you ruminate
until it hits the ground

from point *a* to *b*
the matter travels
through a sea of debris

you see
what starts in your head
weighs most at your feet

the lesson is *no retreat!*
the action –
keep moving.

intuition

what if i told you
what you already knew?

what if i told you
i have some clues

no strings
no dues

a pinch of power
a tincture of truth

are you in
to find out where you've been?

you'll need these keys to love
and a license to sin

hear your heart
go on and listen

change rests in all that's sentient.
pray to the tightness in your chest

and all that was ever meant
here in the present –

see beneath your breath
feel for that first sense.

it's subtle – *yes* – over to the left
next to those stale notes

hidden and well kept
there! grab it!

you jolt awake
weightless again without stake

go ahead in the rain
this is strength after pain

what if you
are all it takes?

unconventionally audible

you don't need ears to listen
in a world of vibrations and patterns

we can learn to listen
with our fingertips

with our hands
and even our cheeks

it's in touch
and much to our discovery

that we can feel for sounds
in ways we smell colours

we don't need a sixth sense
to communicate with each other.

perception

to see the forest
through the trees
is to believe
in more than you see

to feel the ocean
beyond the reef
can sink beliefs
in a sea of needs

to hear beauty
within the beast
is to listen –
entirely.

do what you love

to live each day as your last
with no bookends to your week
no sunday or monday to bind our sleep.

to play each day individually
focusing on little things
contributing to the big thing

fulfillment and *happiness*
(the phone rings)
will you answer?

what would your day look like?
in ways one forms practice in passion
how long will you last and
what if life passes before you can ask?

concerns of survival
to make ends meet
flow from leaky faucets onto the street

is it inherent
in what we are told to be
or who we ought to become?

is this conformance
or do we outrun
ourselves before risking a performance?

to live each day
free within originality
where imagination meets reality

in a world where there's no limit
to how great
or how late you've been
in a life supported by community

should you ever ask of mine –
more dexterity in my hands and feet
creative days under a tree
playing out stories that come to me.

for the love of it

folks don't do things
for the love of it anymore
whatever happened to passion
pursuing what the heart stands for?

money won't settle a score
between an interest and its reward
it can't win over feelings
that depend on back doors either

folks won't do things for nothing
unless told by an advisor.
when did we become hard-core
and further to the touch?

as if being tough is a sign of strength
and society can't get enough –
what is up with this construct?

i never thought as much
until i was caught being the judge
guilty once the hypocrisy pierced
my guts.

sick i was acting somebody else
i went away before coming
back to myself –

the boy who did things
because of how he felt –
and if his heart could melt

it would marinate over music
and words –
something higher than himself.

connected

my skin is calm
in a momentary ease

floating
in an ethereal dream

no reservations
no retreat

above suffering
we're all free

a castaway
from melancholy

enlightened by our humility
i'm focused on this clarity

riding upon humanity
like birds atop a rolling breeze

to see nature in one's being
is all matter and means

an awakened eye will see – in the third degree
i am you and you are me.

rising > < falling

i spent all week rising
and falling with the sun

waking up with nature
before the day has begun

slowing down
after the night has come.

in these moments there's no one
but *her* and me

sweet mother
in all her glory.

worry-free

between two palms
when dusk turns from dawn

waves crash
while the sun hangs long

drunk and warm on song
tonight's muse is strong

all our worries have gone
nothing can go wrong

between
two palms.

let go

to flow freely
in the rhythm of the globe

to sooth that tempered ego
for a moment of fluidity

to forget
what you know

to slow down and question
what you've been told

behind the glitter
beyond the gold

there's only new and old
what is true is already so

to flow freely
mind open or closed.

believe to see

seek the thoughts
you're after

it's no matter

beliefs blossom
from natural disaster.

botanical belief

in a garden of plants and trees
stars lay pressed upon leaves

contained constellations
of botanical belief

each flares without symmetry
individually unique

like the walk to one's step
distinct from another

therein lies the message –
in a star pressed upon a leaf.

way of the mind

try
to occupy

not by talk
but thought

the way of
the mind.

harness the wind

what breathing means to me
normally wouldn't be so obvious

more than ever it seems
the elixir of life is to breathe
and you don't need an audience.

soft and slow
deeply and full

to fill our lungs is to return home
with every breath
an emotion of our own

longing to connect
our spirit with the present
until it can be physically shown

breaking fear from our bones –
breathing opens a window
shining light where shadows grow

this is how i know
harnessing the wind
will save my home.

reflective poetry

belonging to the seasons
with no end in time

expressed in some form
riddled within each line

a story of yours
a story of mine

a memory of you
an undiscovered truth

usually a way in
eventually a way out

acceptance and forgiveness
the *why* and *how*

familiar sounds on new ground
through the ups and downs.

purpose > < place

if i had a clue
about coincidence and truth

or every destiny we're due
i would tell you

life callings come like cards
in pairs until split apart

people's perspectives punch
before we find ourselves to start

what will it be in the end –
for fame or a place in your heart?

serve

it's the words we serve
that influence our worth

too many forces at work
in and outside this earth

it's the words we serve
that deserve praise first

give birth to a meaning
and mold it into a verse

put your ego in a hearse
and don't make it worse.

as we frequent a universe
where pros meet verbs

observe with a thirst
and feel this energy surge

with each and every word
watch your purpose burst.

spirited away

if our time isn't borrowed
would you still fly home?

where love grows modest
and wayward like a comet

if my mind isn't followed
could you go when i go –

blushing like a tomato
do you know what i know?

today and tomorrow
traveling country from metro

city folks grow inaudible
will i ever find my arrow?

feeling spirited away
in fanny bay from toronto –

some land of promise
up and over the rainbow.

what if there was room

what if there was a room
where sunshine begins and moonlight ends?

every day of each night
a room available to you

no check-ins or workarounds
a room fit for two
a space you're always allowed

depending on who's passing through
and what's holding the door

the walls are warm
and have been built and torn
over and over

the callused floor has been worn
again and again

coloured by life's score
and whoever's clutching the pen

this room smells of either lust or lead
it has a past and future
but works best in present tense –

a place encouraging you to live free
but never forget
the binding recipe is mindfulness.

how can you find a room
that does for others
what it can do for you?

this is the big question
i assume

in the attic lay images of war
and sunny afternoons

flowers grow from memories
that are less confused

feelings watered
by something we once knew

this room is where it always starts –
the room inside your heart.

beginnings

the day i forgave myself
was the day i accepted truth

rediscovering
who i already was
and believing in him too.

the road to forgiveness
is difficult to witness
and even harder to do

acknowledging what happened
and still finding a way through

after three years i chose
to address the room –

i kept it secret
as if releasing it
would retire the way i wanted to

be seen
be heard
be understood

what good comes from hiding?
to grow we must break glass ceilings
though it's easy to fold when we're grieving –

this wasn't an option anymore.
i needed to face
what was behind that door

guilt and shame
from my own cold war

trauma upon the shore
from battles i started but never stood for

casualties of conversations
wrapped in passages that read
"you may be fragile but at least you're not dead!"

i resurrected the memory
heavy as the shadow in my head.

i weaved a thread from cause to effect
and said
"if i accept without judgement the stronger i get"

a grand gesture to the heartache in my chest.
with that healing i wept and wept –

it was time to leave behind
what remained left

people will have to see me
for who i am today

sip slow and prosper

i’m the only person that can serve and protect
how i give and get

the day i forgave myself
was the day i learned self-respect

nobody to fear and nothing to fret
free to be in the light i sentenced to death.

my mind finally caught its breath
bullets of regret
returned from where they shot.

through acceptance
i was able to move on
eventually the sabotage stopped.

departure

there's no reason to hurry to the other shore
because we won't get anywhere
until we know what for –

sip slow and prosper.

acknowledgements

i thank my family for teaching us what it means to be loved. lasting gratitude to sarah dunlop who encouraged me to write and understood i must. to everyone who lifts poetry onto its feet and believed mine should be shared – a significant nudge.

poems

sources

thank you rohinton mistry (penguin random house) and kay larson (harper collins) for permission to use quoted material from their books and maryann endanawas from lttb gijigowi language department for the translations in *dearly departed.*

about the author

dylan is a canadian author of poetry. born october 24 1992 he grew up in burlington ontario with his parents and younger sister. in his poems he engages themes of society and self – relationships and mental health. enigmas of the human spirit. his debut collection *sip slow and prosper* is introspective and lyrical in form. a medium for his style of writing. dylan has been living in british columbia since 2014.

website	www.brooksdylan.com
instagram	@babblingbrooksy
email	dylanpatrickbrooks@gmail.com